Religion
AND THE
Variety of
Culture

Christian Mission and Modern Culture

EDITED BY
ALAN NEELY, H. WAYNE PIPKIN,
AND WILBERT R. SHENK

In the series:

Believing in the Future, by David J. Bosch

Write the Vision, by Wilbert R. Shenk

Truth and Authority in Modernity,
by Lesslie Newbigin

Religion and the Variety of Culture,
by Lamin Sanneh

Religion
AND THE
Variety of
Culture

**A Study in Origin
and Practice**

LAMIN SANNEH

TRINITY PRESS INTERNATIONAL
Valley Forge, Pennsylvania

Gracewing.

This volume is a revised and expanded version of Chapter 1 of *Encountering the West: Christianity and the Global Cultural Process: The African Dimension*, published in 1993 by Marshall Pickering in Great Britain and Orbis Books in the United States and Canada. Appreciation is expressed to these publishers for permission to publish it in this revised form.

First published by
TRINITY PRESS INTERNATIONAL
P.O. Box 851
Valley Forge, PA 19482–0851
U.S.A.

First British edition
published by
GRACEWING
2 Southern Avenue
Leominster
Herefordshire HR6 0QF
England

Trinity Press International is part of the Morehouse Publishing Group.

Cover design: Brian Preuss

Library of Congress Cataloging-in-Publication Data

Sanneh, Lamin O.
   Religion and the variety of culture : a study in origin and
practice / Lamin Sanneh. – 1st U.S. ed.
     p. cm. – (Christian mission and modern culture)
   Rev. and expanded version of chapter 1 of Encountering the West.
1993.
   Includes bibliographical references (p.).
   ISBN 1-56338-166-4 (pbk. : alk. paper)
   1. Religion and culture. 2. Christianity and culture.
I. Encountering the West. II. Title. III. Series.
BL65.C8S26 1996
291.1'7–dc20
                        96-8088
                        CIP

Gracewing ISBN 0-85244-378-1

Printed in the United States of America

96   97   98   99   00   01   6   5   4   3   2   1

Contents

Preface to the Series

Both Christian mission and modern culture, widely regarded as antagonists, are in crisis. The emergence of the modern mission movement in the early nineteenth century cannot be understood apart from the rise of technocratic society. Now, at the end of the twentieth century, both modern culture and Christian mission face an uncertain future.

One of the developments integral to modernity was the way the role of religion in culture was redefined. Whereas religion had played an authoritative role in the culture of Christendom, modern culture was highly critical of religion and increasingly secular in its assumptions. A sustained effort was made to banish religion to the backwaters of modern culture.

The decade of the 1980s witnessed further momentous developments on the geopolitical front with the collapse of communism. In the aftermath of the breakup of the system of power blocs that dominated international relations for a generation, it is clear that religion has survived even if its institutionalization has undergone deep change and its future forms are unclear. Secularism continues to oppose religion, while technology has emerged as a major source of power and authority in modern culture. Both confront Christian faith with fundamental questions.

The purpose of this series is to probe these developments from a variety of angles with a view to helping the church understand its missional responsibility to a culture in crisis. One important resource is the church's experience of two centuries of cross-cultural mission that has reshaped the church into a global Christian *ecumene*. The focus of our inquiry will be the church in modern culture. The series (1) examines modern/postmodern culture from a missional point of view; (2) develops the theological agenda that the church in modern culture must address in order to recover its own integrity; and (3) tests fresh conceptualizations of the nature and mission of the church as it engages modern culture. In other words, these volumes are intended to be a forum where conventional assumptions can be challenged and alternative formulations explored.

This series is a project authorized by the Institute of Mennonite Studies, research agency of the Associated Mennonite Biblical Seminary, and supported by a generous grant from the Pew Charitable Trusts.

Editorial Committee

ALAN NEELY
H. WAYNE PIPKIN
WILBERT R. SHENK

Introduction

We in the West are heirs to a curious paradox concerning Christianity and Western culture. Modern Christianity, in transmitting the message of the Bible through the mother tongue, has encouraged the development of preliterate cultures in the non-Western world.[1] In the West, however, a firm disavowal of the positive reciprocity of religion and culture persists. Western conceptions of culture have, in general, promoted distrust of religion. This is partly the consequence of the often justified critique of mission as cultural imperialism. It is also the consequence of Enlightenment thinking, in which culture became the rule for secular disaffection with religion. When carried over to non-Western contexts, however, the culture-religion dichotomy of the West fails to account for the extraordinary movements of cultural renewal taking place under the shadow of Christianity in non-Western countries. Modern Western concepts of culture thus become a stumbling block to understanding the fruitful convergence of religion and culture currently taking place in non-Western societies.

In this volume I will examine the origins of the culture-religion dichotomy in the West. I will assess the religious interest in culture and the forms that culture took in harboring and propagating anti-religious sentiments. In the second stage of the analysis, I want to restate the theological initiative for elucidating the cultural process and to call attention to the rich cross-cultural resources now available to us in world Christianity.

It was as a rival contender with religious faith that culture was formally introduced to me. This was the lot of most of my generation of American undergraduates who had been exposed to the "cultural relativism" of Ruth Benedict's *Patterns of Culture.* For many of us, culture was the grand strategy by which to bring down Christianity, or at least the Christianity we associated with missionary ambition. (In its extreme form, such contentions come quite close to cultural fundamentalism, which is nearly as implacable as its religious analogue — in part because the cultural critic evokes and begets his or her religious foe, and in part because cultural moralization hardens in its own defense.) It did not occur to us to ask whether the cultural case against Christianity and the a priori rejection of reciprocity between cultures had any merit, so potent was the ferment that galvanized the ranks. In that setting, evidence, or a semblance of it, could prove but one thing — the scale of religious mischief.

For a long time all of us thus affected found ourselves preempted by the reigning shibboleths — our straightforward lines of inquiry and understanding broken by high-profile ideological stakes supported by unshakable confidence in the power of human reason. We were stampeded into acquiescence by this confidence in rationality, held hostage in a closed Newtonian universe that fostered the same law of causality that the social sciences would apply to human motive, behavior, and conduct. This state of affairs came about not just because scholars accidentally stumbled upon reason like an undiscovered galaxy; it was because they began with religion as obscurantist and tyrannical, with reason as the weapon in that combat rather than reason as a neutral tool. It led to a scientific humanism that eventually would percolate through much of the non-Western world, including Africa, thanks to European colonial ascendancy and the academic tradition it spawned. Thus did scientific anthropology collar so-called primitive religions by the principles and rules of observation, description, and explanation, conceiving of the relation between belief and society as a control system with a negative feedback. Accordingly, religion was viewed as a social device that restrained uncharitable behavior; but the negative feedback allowed for the harmless discharge of anxiety and grudge. It is an approach that would not spare classical Christianity, confronting the churches with a challenge they could not suppress, however differently they might resolve it.

It is fair to interject, however, that Enlightenment rationalism was predicated on a spiritual, intellectual commitment, on a willingness to trust and commend certain critical principles on the basis that they would achieve for us the freedom and progress deemed necessary for human fulfillment. The whole procedure amounted to unquestioned faith that "man," not God, was in charge of human destiny. With the center thus crumbling under the impact of scientific rationalism and the flanks occupied, religious believers had nowhere to turn. If they turned to the left they were met with a rampant, single-minded reductionism of the gospel, and to the right they were greeted with avatars of cultural elitism. The question, then, was how to respond (1) to the moral universalism of the left and (2) to the right's insistence on religious uniqueness and with it national grandeur of the kind that is sealed with divine favor; and in either case how to do so over the gauntlet thrown down by rational criticism. With that catch-22 we felt ourselves religiously and culturally disenfranchised.

I recall my professor of French, a self-avowed child of the French Enlightenment, tweaking my nose because I represented for him what he called "religious mystification in an age of reason."[1] He loved driving; and it was not, he teased, divine power that made his motor car perform but premium grade capitalist gasoline. Because he had the upper hand, my choice in class was to submit or else have him flunk me — but on what grounds? Living in that world as children of a different culture, my friends and I had no idea what had hit us, except we felt dizzy from the cultural assault, reduced to deference in the intimidating shadow of those who knew better. In the secret of our hearts, however, we persisted for a sign.

Many of my college superiors were comfortable with the knowledge that they had figured out the world, that not much of surprise remained within the realm of possibility to upset their equilibrium, and that a warm, genial rationality in which human beings found their own answers to life's questions would become the universal condition for all people. The liberal arts curriculum, adjusted, if need be, to accommodate new knowledge, was the fundamental catechism for this enlightened dispensation. The basic forms and conditions of human fulfillment were seen to have been put in place — a human fulfillment in which religion was accounted for and superseded. Individual contentment replaced all inherited tradition and systems. The rule was to claim such contentment as the goal of all effort in order to go beyond norms of conformity and community obligation.

I believe the cultural project should not, indeed cannot, avoid moral judgment simply by claiming a limited, relative ground for itself. The historian who claims impartiality will illumine the field using the categories "righteous" and "unrighteous." Denying the distinction altogether precludes any evaluation even of historical events. Exchanging appreciation of other cultures with skepticism and repudiation of one's own leads us to accord to other cultures prerogatives we repudiated in ourselves. It is difficult to see how a cultural project, defined in the hard terms of self-distrust, can help but duplicate the parodies it noisily identified in religion or how it can survive the habit formed in denying one's heritage.[2]

Our teachers too were firmly locked into the prevailing cultural attitudes. There was little incentive to look beyond the West for contrasting idioms. I recall, for example, how in my philosophy classes there was little willingness to hear counterarguments to current views on material and psychological determinism. Aristotle was psychologized and operationalized to produce a mechanical, autonomous system. His structure of "four" causes was collapsed and his teleology hobbled. We found it easy to dismiss any notion of moral purpose and the need for interpersonal ethics. I do not personally remember any of our professors teaching us about truth, trust, duty, and service to others. We were taught that we made ourselves as we acted, or did not act, in pursuit of expressive goals and could otherwise live or vegetate without profit to anyone else. However, in our hearts we knew better.

I found much later, to my relief, that we did not have to capitulate to material or psychological determinism to affirm the cultural project, especially in its global setting. My task here is to show how that is so and, in doing that, to follow in the footsteps of writers like Ernst Troeltsch and Lesslie Newbigin.

1

The Cultural Critique

In their very different ways, Sir James Frazer (1854–1941) and Lucien Levy-Bruhl (1857–1939)[3] agree that superstition and prelogical thinking (what Levy-Bruhl controversially calls "mystical collective representations of society") characterize the world-view of tribal peoples and constitute their religion. The views of these scholars are typical of the current that has carried the spurt of evolutionary thinking into the battle against religion. In the context of evolutionary thinking, progress was conceived as a staged development from magic to religion to science. Frazer stated tersely that religion is "the despair of magic and merely succeeds it in time." Magic was conceived as the crude, primitive form religion took in prescientific societies whose primitive mentality, Levy-Bruhl argued, interposed a collective subjective mystical layer on all sense perceptions. Another modern writer speaks of magic as nothing but "mysticism in the fetters of fixed idea" (Oman 1931:384).

We may thus take Frazer and Levy-Bruhl as representative of those who believe natural causation to be the root of reality and the grounds for objective knowledge.

We may quibble with this view on two grounds. First, our evolutionary notions result in a demotion, a stereotype, or at any rate a denial that the past played any meaningful role in shaping our views today. Second, we may encourage by our attitudes an ideological willfulness in restricting the word *magical* to negative presuppositions — obscurantism as opposed to progress, slavery rather than freedom — and thus ignore what the word may have meant to those who used it.

2

Magic in the Renaissance

To the writers of the Renaissance it is true that magic and science stood at nearly opposite ends of the spectrum, but it was never remotely their intention to equate magic with obscurantism and science with progress, the one with slavery and the other with freedom, in the manner we have done today. Rather the reverse is true. For them, magic stood for freedom and progress, whereas science represented fatalism and absolute dogma.[4] If the Renaissance thinkers had no one else as their inspiration, they would still have been keen to recruit magic for their enterprise in pursuit of a humane, compassionate world order, a sentiment expressed by Prospero in Shakespeare's *The Tempest*. Although he lives in a cave on an isolated island, Prospero turns one of his apartments into a study where he keeps books "which chiefly treated of magic, a study at that time much affected by all learned men; and the knowledge of this art he found very useful to him" (Lamb n.d.: 1). For that age, science, given its unbending, immutable laws and principles of causation, actually enslaved human beings with the fetters of natural causation.[5] On the other hand, as Francis Bacon put it, when magic was shorn of "centaurs and chimeras," it would bring us to the position where, in Dürer's words, "men can do if they will."[6]

Thus magic became identified with freedom, and science with determinism. And determinism in the age of the Enlightenment was fixed in frigid cosmic space, with human destiny left at the behest of blinking stars and gyrating planets beyond the reach or influence of people. This view found its way into theology, with Ficino, for example, arguing that planetary bodies exert an influence on human beings: they affect "the soul, and move it through that [human] spirit which the Physicians often call the bond of the soul and body" (Walker 1958:48). Others found support in the works of Thomas Aquinas, who taught that God rules in everything through the stars, though free will might be exempt from this astral determinism (:57, 214ff). In science, especially the form assimilated in "bad" astrology, our fate hangs on nonsentient, invisible, and invincible forces whose natural impact on our minds is to reduce us to futility. The mind is thus reduced to the category of a physical organ, its hidden form an argument for reducing it to a subunit of natural contingency.[7]

Scientific determinism was intolerable for all con-
cerned. For thinkers like Del Rio and Telesio, scientific culture needed to be rescued from blind conformity and made amenable to human experience and
instrumentality. That human beings could partici-
pate meaningfully in the cumulative construction of
the universe was the overriding proof and burden of
magic as Renaissance science understood it, because
progress as "cumulative construction" is an issue of
moral teleology, not simply a mechanistic or logis-
tical matter. It was under the influence of "magic"
that "the scientists and inventors of the seventeenth
century reveal a breath-taking faith in the potentialities of human ingenuity" (Thomas 1971:662). In
its creative stage "magic" was prominent by its use,
not its abuse. Scientists saw in the cycle of calcu-
lation, enumeration, measurement, observation, and
description — what one critic called the ideological
penumbra of "the magic of numbers, the fetish of
quantification, the self-defeating quest for certainty
in matters sublunary" (Porter 1992:20) — room for
moral purpose and human partnership.

At its simplest, writers believed that the new science should be a servant, not master, of humans.
Bacon, therefore, urged that the new knowledge be
sought for the power it puts into our hands rather
than as an end in itself. It should be, in his words,
"a spouse for fruit," not a "curtesan [*sic*] for pleasure"
(Lewis 1954:14).

Given all this, our attitude today of binding magic to religion and bringing them in their shared defect to the butchering block of science is too abrupt a break from the motives of Renaissance authors for whom the objective chain of natural causation does not bind more securely on the basis that a subjective religious chain of disrepute be first unscrambled, however dialectically satisfying that may be.

3

Enlightenment and Romantic Views

This resolve of writers to place human beings at the forefront of affairs produced an intellectual breakthrough in the contemporary conception of "man." Medieval Christian theology had viewed the human being as a composite creature, an *animal rationale,* in whose power it lay to be governed by reason or animality. Such a choice, however, was circumscribed by limits set by God: we could become saints but not angels, brutes but not beasts. In other words, the boundary between the moral order and the natural world was strictly drawn, whatever the latitude available to us as moral agents. It was this distinction that defined the medieval notion of culture. It was to suffer a massive retrenchment in the shift afoot in Enlightenment thinking.

The new view departed from the old in a radical way. Pico della Mirandola (1463–94), a Renaissance scientist who defended magic, said that the human being has no specific nature but creates one by his or her own acts. He put the following words into God's mouth:

> To thee, O Adam, We have giuen no certain habitation or countenance of thine owne neither anie peculiar office, so that what habitation or countenance or office soeuer thou dost choose for thyselfe, the same thou shalt enjoye and posses at thine owne proper will and election. We haue made thee neither a thing celestial nor a thing terrestrial, neither mortal nor immortal, so that being thine owne fashioner and artificer of thyselfe, thou maist make thyselfe after what likenes thou dost most affecte" (Lewis 1954:13).

Another writer of the period places "man" in this indeterminate position, throwing off the earlier certainty of the old limits and its theological anchor. This writer says, "man containeth in himself the stars and the heauen, they lie hidden in his minde . . . if we rightly knew our owne spirite no thing at all would be impossible to us on earth" (:16).[8]

Bacon's buoyant confidence is driven by this sense of new possibilities open to human beings as human beings rather than as natural adjuncts, a confidence upheld by the idea of a purposeful creation and our moral stewardship for it. True knowledge, he says, is a "rich storehouse for the glory of the Creator and the relief of man's estate." He continues, "Let no man... think or maintain that a man can search too far or be too well studied in the book of God's word, or in the book of God's works, divinity or (natural) philosophy; but rather let men endeavor an endless progression in both: only let men beware that they apply both to charity, and not to swelling; to use and not to ostentation" (Wightman 1972:159).[9] Faith and science for him were allies, though he cautioned it would be unwise "to mingle or confound these learnings together." Yet neither did he intend to oppose them to each other, because God's designs, he felt, may be discovered in nature by a knowledge of the "chain of causes" that "cannot by any force be loosed or broken nor can nature be commanded except by being obeyed" (Klaaren 1985:92–93). In a work published in 1603 called *The Masculine Birth of Time,* subtitled "The Great Instauration of the Dominion of Man over the Universe," Bacon appended a petitionary prayer in which he prayed that "our human interests may not stand in the way of the divine, nor from the unlocking of the paths of sense" (:92–93; Trevor-Roper 1967:186f).

In the classical Enlightenment definition of culture, this theme of confidence in a purposeful creation and its corollary of human instrumentality and moral agency forms an animating and coherent principle of the cultural project. As such the life of the mind plays a preponderant and central role. As a consequence, the door was open to the triumph of human self-sufficiency and to the cultivation of inner autonomy and intellectual harmony as superior, or at any rate as prior to the practical efforts of production and industry.[10]

A later extreme Enlightenment trend saw culture as one in which all valid intellectual projects are facets of Bacon's perfect "globe of knowledge," a rigid formalism that encouraged blind rationalism, or else a static natural religion in which the leading figures were Hobbes in naturalistic ethics, Locke in natural reason, and Grotius in natural rights. Consequently, a reaction ensued with the Counter-Enlightenment, whose leaders felt called upon to repudiate the static tendencies of their forerunners and to retrieve the issue of culture-consciousness as a problem for their own age. The rigid conceptualism of Enlightenment thought about culture received some softening with the appropriation of aesthetics. Thus the idealization of beauty was added to the exaltation of reason to make room for sentiment. Nevertheless, aesthetic appreciation began itself to freeze cultural forms, as writers looked to what might be characteristic norms or general types, all of this somewhat removed from the subjective, intuitive capacity. Lessing (1780) gave this rationalistic aspect a strong emphasis, as did Winckelmann, who expressed it well when he said "beauty should be like the purest water, which, the less taste it has, is regarded as the most healthful because it is free from foreign elements" (Winckelmann 1808–25:Bk IV, Ch II, #23).

With Kant we reach an important turning point between the Enlightenment view of culture and the Romantic view. In his *Critique of Pure Reason* (1781), Kant gives philosophical reasons for abandoning the classical Enlightenment account of culture. He wrote that "metaphysics is the completion of the whole culture of reason." Yet it was in his *Critique of Judgement* (1790) that Kant propounded a new aesthetic theory on beauty and taste to the effect that aesthetic appreciation is based on "that which pleases universally without requiring a concept" (1951:77ff), a proposition that understands culture to be nothing but the intellectual life in imaginative free play. At one stroke Kant removed culture from any transcendent religious norms,[11] and, equally momentously, like Hegel, sundered culture from all local, mother tongue moorings.[12] Kant established for culture its own system of transcendentalism that was to have enormous impact on the Romantic school of philosophy and poetry as well as on Schiller's distinction between the theoretical, practical, and aesthetic (moral, physical, and aesthetical) facets of culture.

Schiller (1793) was occupied by two main ideas, namely, the ideal of humanity as ethical and the fact of human beings as creatures of sense. Schiller uses aesthetics to mediate between the extremes of sense impression and ethical idealism, although in fact Schiller moderates, if he does not abandon, his confidence in culture as understood by the Enlightenment by turning to nature for final vindication. Feelings and sentiments grounded in nature acquired in Schiller's scheme a status higher than culture as something constructed. Virtue for Schiller resides in nature, whereas culture is tainted with evil.[13]

The next paradigmatic shift to natural realism was carried to rhapsodic heights by Nietzsche, with his dethronement of spirit and truth and their replacement with the culture of egoistic nihilism and activism. In this new realism, writers were quick to notice the appealing distinction drawn by Schopenhauer between will and intellect, or will and spirit (Schopenhauer 1969:25). Passion became the source and shaper of values. Wagner expresses this idea in a letter to August Rockel in 1854 about his opera *Siegfried:* "Wotan rises to the tragic height of willing his own downfall. This is all we have to learn from the history of Man — to will the necessary and ourselves to bring it to pass." With that act Wotan becomes the unacknowledged patron saint of the superegoist. With Wagner, Nietzsche, and others like them, the modern West turned its back on the Apollonian assurances of tradition and launched precariously into the Dionysiac culture of will and defiance.

This is the culture of Max Stirner, Zola, Ibsen, Turgenieff, and, in the United States, of Emerson

(1803–82) and Poe (1809–49), among others.[14] In their own ways, Poe and Ibsen harp on a common cultural theme, that having to do with the morbid and mysterious and the sense of conflict or alienation. Their works represent an attempt to objectify in a fresh medium the depths of the human soul, a culture-consciousness of the decadent and vicious in human life. Nevertheless, in seeking to express the shadow side of culture, both Poe and Ibsen have also introduced a critical note, with culture being assessed not in the "naive" and transcendental terms of the Romantics, but in the hard, despairing mood of the post-Realists.

Today the culture of deconstruction and of deconstructionists, although liberating us from old conformities and conventions, might tie us to new orthodoxies of distrust and alienation. New cultural projects leave us with old questions and suspicions. We continue to face the problem, for example, of how we adjudicate ultimate issues of truth and justice with the relative tools of deconstruction, how to move from existential questions of sense and sensibility to normative principles of equity and service to each other. Therefore, we may ask: Can the human instrument, without a sense of transcendence, achieve a fulfillment that is different from murky self-centeredness? What is to prevent intellectual egoism from becoming a creed for self-centeredness? What is to distinguish nihilism and egoism, for instance, from dogmatic subjectivism or liberal fantasy? What moral imperatives can check these unwholesome tendencies of life and thought? How do we intellectually and institutionally cater for this moral view of life? Does obedience in "nature," to employ Bacon's terms, presume its analogue in a higher obedience? Is culture-consciousness complete without the prior consciousness rooted in God, a consciousness that brings the creative impulse into manifest harmony with its divine prevenience?

Such ultimate and normative criteria require a re-appraisal of the autonomous claims for culture, and require a synthesis that would take out of the equation the old battlelines between contingency and teleology, between the imperatives of moral reasoning and the episodic facts of the cultural and contemplative life.[15]

We cannot, I think, be satisfied with a merely mechanistic and materialist notion of culture. A purely mechanistic or instrumental view of culture — that is, a concern only with culture as a subject of organization and administration — brings us inescapably to the problem of culture as a contest of national wills and individual endowment, with culture theory serving to promote a sentiment of cultural destiny and imperial grandeur. This has obvious implications for the cultures of weaker nations, not to say anything of the disadvantaged classes in the West itself.

The problem is actually made even more acute if we idealize language and empty it of all content, such as we find in Winckelmann's statement that culture, like beauty, "should be like the purest water, which, the less taste it has, is regarded as the most healthful because it is free from foreign elements." This sort of abstraction is what provoked John Ruskin (1819–1900) to complain of modern art as "the graceful emptiness of representation" in regard to which religious subjects are exploited "for the display of transparent shadows, skilful tints, and scientific foreshortenings . . . and academical discrimination" (Herbert 1964:260). When culture has been thus dissolved and distilled into Kantian ideals of "universal pleasure," it leaves in place an elite corps of cultural arbiters whose sensibilities determine the course of evolutionary development from primitive forms to abstract conceptions. Yet no abstract refined formulation should make us forget the stage when the noble character of common speech falls on our ears with the fresh spontaneity of lived experience, unmediated by formal categories. Such was the complaint of Troeltsch when he wrote, with Kant not far from his mind, that

> as far as this creative life is concerned, it is impossible, at least *a posteriori*, to strip away the particularity of a given phenomenon and then distill from the remainder a concealed but

operative universal. The impossibility of pro-
ceeding in this way is shown by the fact that
the idea of a universal, wherever it arises, is itself brought into being in terms of particular
historical conditions. It can arise only by effecting what becomes a historically necessary
departure from the living content that dominated whatever form preceded it, and it always
takes shape in relation to definite intellectual
and ethical influences of a given situation and
moment (Troeltsch 1971:64).

In that connection, a study of Elizabethan life
found that the ordinary, humbler folk possessed the
creative spark that fired the wider cultural impulse,
so that "the art of the higher regions of society
was most strongly influenced by the vigor in the
cultural activities of the common people in their
popular pageants, folk songs and dances" (Meyer
1946, cited in Tawney 1966:208). This is one reason why it could be said of the art of John Bunyan
that it "reeks heavily of the soil, and is not ashamed
of its origins" (208), because, as C. S. Lewis puts
it, Bunyan's "homely immediacy" may be attributed
to "a perfect natural ear, a great sensibility for the
idiom and cadence of popular speech, a long experience in addressing unlettered audiences" (Lewis
1979:146–53).
The circularity of thought involved with the ab-

straction of culture, with using a specific idiom to advocate an abstract universal idea, would render the whole cultural project doubtful unless we allowed the specificity of idiom as "foreign elements" a role in culture-consciousness. For then, Western formulations themselves, "foreign" by the standards of others, would acquire a validity on the basis of their own cultural specificity. That is why, to amend John Keats, certain kinds of philosophy, in stripping culture so completely, would also clip the wings of angels, for even refined imagination requires to be clothed in the language and circumstance of historical conditionality. A universal language, in that case, may not dispense with the innumerable rules and forms and characteristics that constitute the bones and sinews of cultural particularity. Similarly, we do not get universal culture merely by abolishing or merging the tones and sounds bequeathed to us by the uncountable vessels and arteries of custom, convention, and rules of observance. Stripped of those means and circumstances, culture has little solidity, though it may be a category of intellectual abstraction — what Butler called "the entertainment of the mind" (*Sermons*, XV).

4

Modern Attitudes

It is perhaps inevitable that the upholders of a materialist doctrine of culture should fall into a narrow ideological trap, preaching freedom, progress, and reason with the commitment fired by opposition to religion. This problem became ever more pressing in the 1930s and 40s. Thus we find Joseph Stalin, not in other ways a salutary figure, expressing a sentiment that lies at the heart of the Western experience. He made the cultural project a matter for instrumental control, with the nation as its embodiment. In that connection he said that a nation "is a historically evolved, stable community of language, territory, economic life, and psychological makeup manifested in a common culture." A modern commentator remarked: "Put a centralized government on top of that, allow for neutralized monarchs to remain in place where the populace retains a lingering respect for royalty, and you have the kind of modern country with which we are all familiar" (Lawday 1991:22). But national loyalty begs the moral question: Is the nation final arbiter of our moral responsibility? The nation as moral agent might produce the sort of sentiment that led a British army officer then fighting the Nazis to say to a German anti-Nazi victim of Hitler after the victim fled to Britain: "I can respect no man who has no loyalty to his country, especially the country of his birth" (Gillman 1980:230).

Mussolini made an even bolder and more direct claim when he taunted Christians with observing that the religion would have remained what he termed "a wretched little oriental sect" in an undistinguished corner of the world had not the Italian cultural genius "salvaged" it from an almost certain demise and raised it above the floodmark (Toynbee 1957:92–93). It was thus that Italy's chief city, Rome, carved its name on the church that became a worldwide body. More than a whiff of such sentiments exists within the church itself. On the occasion of Mussolini's invasion of Ethiopia in October 1935, the bishop of Cremona consecrated the regimental flags and declared: "The blessing of God be upon these soldiers who, on African soil, will conquer new and fertile lands for the Italian genius, thereby bringing to them Roman and Christian culture" (Hastings 1987:314). Similarly, Cardinal Schuster of Milan hailed the Italian army for being destined to achieve "the triumph of the Cross ... opening the gates of Abyssinia to the Catholic faith and civilization" (:314).[16]

The views of Stalin and Mussolini in this and other matters are, of course, extreme, but they represent a phenomenon that in its moderate forms has characterized the spread and expansion of Christianity, for on the face of it the Enlightenment national state and the Christian cultural assimilation are undeniable facts, however lamentable in either case some aspects may be. What is different now is that both Stalin and Mussolini are feeding off the long-standing legacy of the cultural project as an anti-Christian project, and in riding the crest of cultural triumphalism, they articulate a corresponding radical emasculation of religion. From now on, whenever we see or hear of Western cultural contact with non-Western societies, we can only assume violence and imperialism as the basis and logic of the encounter, precisely the view Joseph Conrad expressed in *The Heart of Darkness,* and it takes little imagination to understand how Western Christian missions filled this role. Stalin and Mussolini, however, had their allies where it counted, in the political project of the architects of wartime Europe. The new masters of the scene followed a theory of culture that rests on the split-level foundation of biology and force. The first provides the natural advantage of racial superiority, while the second provides the instrument of its effectiveness.

Thus could Alfred Rosenberg, the theorist of National Socialism, argue in favor of Aryan cultural superiority, because for him "culture is determined mostly by biology, so that one ethnic group's acceptance of another's cultural legacy [i.e., northern Europe's adoption of a Jewish-influenced Christianity] is unnatural and takes place only because of violence.... If the cultural system is already implicit in the biological self (i.e., the body), then any large-scale cultural shift, such as the Christianization of northern Europe, must be altogether owing to domination and in no sense the result of the greater persuasiveness of the new order" (Levenson 1991:17). Rosenberg's method of seeking cultural ascendancy over what he considered the Jewish conspiracy drove him to repudiate the Jewish connections of the New Testament, with his wholesale condemnation of the doctrines of humility, self-denial, and peacefulness as Jewish distortions of the genius of Christianity. The cultural values Rosenberg wanted to promote are determined by blood and affinity, although it is evident biological ideas alone are too haphazard not to require even a warped moral web to unify them. "Unless," as Lewis says, "the measuring rod is independent of the things measured, we can do no measuring," including the pernicious enumeration of racial advantages (Lewis 1967:73; cf. Mill 1958).

The movement that began in the Enlightenment with the courageous and joyful celebration of the

emancipation of the human spirit saw itself as opposed to Christianity, though its faith and vision
derived from the religion. However, in trying to out-
rival Christianity, this immense cultural movement
became in the twentieth century a distorted replica
of its religious foe and degenerated into a partisan
crusade centered on race and nation.

In the first place, intercultural contact was reduced to nothing more than a biologically conceived
self-interest, with force, or at any rate the means
for success, the ruling principle in human relations.
The problem of excess of culture thus turned on
Dionysiac dichotomies in culture. In the second,
science and technology, stripped of all moral stewardship, produced or promoted vested interests, and
the instruments for protecting them, that vied with
Baconian and Kantian assurances. Both the destructive and the diversionary entertainment culture of
modern science and industry encouraged the ascendancy of will over intellect, making acquisitive
desires and goals more than adequate substitutes
for intellectual pleasure and, indeed, bringing the
progress — and decline — of humanity within the
general scope of industrial competence. For the great
dictum of Horace, adopted by Kant, "Know thyself,"
military industrial culture, the technopolis, substi-
tuted "Make thyself," a shift threatening to swamp
us with effluents of rampant consumerism. Thus
the problem persists: our commitment to the cul-

tural project as such is too deeply intertwined with our original affinity with the ultimate moral order to leave us entirely unaffected with regard to spiritual values. On the positive side, this Enlightenment cultural movement has produced imperishable testaments of human creativity, scientific exploration, personal courage, and the discourse of rational argument, though on the negative side it has brought the human spirit into unspeakable agony and moral confusion. The costs of this negative side have now threatened to undo the positive benefits, unless we reject the ideology of cultural innocence and human autonomy.

So long as culture continues to make a bid for the ground properly occupied by religion, so long will we continue to have an alienating hostility embedded in the cultural project, all of which points to an acute crisis in the nature of values and truth. Freud's observation is relevant here, namely, that cultural ideals and what is achieved by them incite cultural superiority. "In this way," Freud claims, "cultural ideals become a source of discord and enmity between different cultural units, as can be seen most clearly in the case of nations" (Freud 1961:13). A triumphant culture, we know only too well, is by no stretch of the imagination synonymous with moral rectitude,[17] nor, for example, is the historical failure of vanquished populations evidence simply of their moral inferiority. Many cultures have triumphed both as ideas and movements that have also wrought great misery in the world, and many other cultures have been trampled upon whose fate, in continuing to go unchallenged, has diminished our capacity for truth.

There is, in fact, no neutral ground in culture, for every inch is contested, say, between egoism and dogmatism, between possessing and betraying, but in any case held *sub judice* to interests and suppositions that are themselves forms of commitment. Cultural forms often assume qualitative values, and description turns into evaluation, with the rules of prescription and preference controlling the perception of what is out there. We should, therefore, admit that "culture is not an ethically neutral entity, and cultural change cannot be a matter of ethical indifference" (Newbigin 1981:161). In this matter, too, we would be wrong to insist on a rigid dichotomy between so-called cultural facts and cultural values; between cultural patterns and configurations on the one hand, and, on the other, moral sentiments and standards. Our very apprehension of the natural world is never so detached that it is not imbued with moral impressions, and this is more so in the cultural domain that the religious shadow overhangs, so that, contrary to Hume's skepticism, we may remedy an agnostic empiricism with what Troeltsch calls the a priori of reason, or what Newbigin calls teleology.

Something of this teleology may act as a prescriptive rule to mitigate and illuminate entropic contradictions within cultures.[18] Thus systemic breakdown would be preempted or mitigated by a moral safety valve that allows the two opposite streams — the one being prescribed, or even normative behavior, and the other forbidden conduct — to meet without permanent harm. Some examples: incest might be a major offense for which horrendous sanctions apply, but the rules of consanguinity might be flexible enough to make second-cousin incest less serious than incest between first cousins or siblings. Similarly, fertility laws might be extremely stringent, so stringent that barrenness, especially if it should become common, might threaten an unacceptably large number of people with a form of social death, in which case the definition of fertility would be expanded to incorporate a more flexible rule of adoption of nieces and nephews and other collateral relatives.[19] In those ways a culture would take steps to devise conceptual and qualitative equivalents for social and biological relationship.

Thus would a culture act to resolve what Bernard Williams calls "the Archimedean point," namely, a species of skepticism that turns out to be unreasonable, or at any rate untenable (Williams 1985:22–29). That is why we cannot take literally what George Orwell said in a different connection, namely, that ethical skepticism has "exploded a hundred tons of dynamite beneath the moralist position, and we are still living in the echo of that tremendous crash" (Orwell 1953:65), because all such skepticism would, at least in meaningful community life, be mitigated by a response of social realism. More than an echo of a similar moral realism still suffuses our consciousness. Consider the extreme case of the community of ancient Israelites, who, in a pinch, would rather go to the Philistines to have their swords sharpened than give up the struggle entirely.

There may, therefore, be an important clue (and it is only as clue that I pursue the subject here) in the fact that as human beings we continue to believe in the progress of humanity through qualities of humaneness, compassion, philanthropy, generosity, peace, and tolerance, making those among the chief attributes of the cultural project, thus invoking the moral ethos shadowing the cultural enterprise as such. The Promethean cultural rebirth we thus seek hints sufficiently at a loss we suffered at an earlier time to make retrieval a moral issue rather than a matter only of natural mutation. It is thus reasonable to conclude that our projects of retrieval require as a goal the moral rehabilitation of the human species, and they leave us as the subject matter of the rehabilitation and the agents for effecting it. This double role should result in a corresponding double awareness, and thus in an important break from the chain of natural causation. The flaw we perceive in the cultural scheme is not simply a missing piece in our biological equipment but a sense that by and in ourselves something is missing, that our wish for cultural deliverance is symptom of a redeemable insecurity in our primordial unconscious, something so profoundly embedded in the roots of being and so wide-ranging in its consequences that we propagate it in the stem and branches of everything we construct, and must thus confront it at its source. That source is our unique and precious affinity with the sovereign moral law.

Therefore the challenge we face in culture is not so much that of empirical completeness, of the accumulation of physical data and the extension of technological mastery, as of an acute sense that our empirical rationalism seems to have its tendrils hedged with a moral screen, rough-hew them how we will. How can our empirical tree flourish when its roots are so entangled? If cultural purpose amounts to anything more than quantitative measures, and the human enterprise more than the sum of its biological functions, then we are right to include spiritual and intellectual activity in our descriptive inventory, to rate gravity concealed below and behind the roots as of equal moment as the elements above. Our cultural jungle is penetrated by trails that would bring us finally to our moral sense, though at present we feel exhausted, and fulfilled, in individually designed tasks of orienteering that bring us back to where it found us.

Indeed the phenomenon that has accompanied the rise of culture consciousness is henotheist faith, of belief in culture as the source of ultimate values, so that although belief in the supernatural has declined or, which is perhaps more common, has come under attack, faith of a less self-interested kind has moved in to take its place. Consequently, the total number of believers and nonbelievers may not have changed much; what has changed significantly has been the relative position of the two categories, with modern cultural believers and religious skeptics reversing roles with their premodern predecessors. Just as believers of a different era took for granted the plausibility of their worldview, so cultural protagonists today assume a corresponding plausibility for their presuppositions. Neither side can afford to doubt what it believes in.

Such certainty is the hard crust under which the moral life finds refuge, with the nonreligious person drawing from such moral reserves without accountability. When our intellectual guides prescribe for us the confidence of humanism, the fatalism of realism, or the despair of naturalism, in fact they are leaving in place this sense that their description is morally evocative, even provocative, that cultural diagnosis includes a yearning for moral truth, that erosion and sedimentation in culture are symbols of fatigue and renewal that evoke death and resurrection and the glorious consummation. It is not adequate with regard to our destiny that we grin and bear it, curse and resist, or else grasp and transcend the flux, but that we understand our response to be a reading of the "facts" guided by intelligence not originated in "facts." At the point where our thoughts and actions are dissected by the forces of life, we have to respond in ways that preserve and promote our authentic selfhood and humanity. We cannot afford at such moments the luxury of detached skepticism and objective disengagement.

Thus we have the case of Einstein, who dropped his pacifism, once fervently held, when faced with Hitler and his horrors, and who relinquished, or at any rate modified, his abhorrence of nationalism when confronted with the demand for a Jewish national state in Israel. Even as a scientist, Einstein drew no dogmatic line between rational demonstration and imaginative insight, convinced, for example, that the comprehensibility of the universe is the greatest of mysteries. The point has been well made that ethical skepticism is very different from skepticism about the material world, for the "ethical involves more, a whole network of considerations, and the ethical skeptic could have a life that ignored such considerations altogether" (Williams 1985:25).

This is one of the reasons the methods of rational demonstration cannot, I believe, take the full measure of culture, for, as Arnold has shown, culture is at heart a spiritual phenomenon, a matter of inner intention. I do not think, furthermore, that the issue lies in psychological moods, with mental orientation able to resolve the difficulty. The psychoanalytic approach to the issue of human happiness might, for instance, explore human character in terms of moods, such as optimism, depression, alienation, fear, gloom, contentment, gratification, and so forth, without in any way relating that to ethical questions. A sadistic person, we recall, might enjoy inflicting suffering on others, his mood at the time being one characteristically of accomplished satisfaction. If we made mood the only criterion of character, it would not help us to differentiate between good and bad or right and wrong; a person may be successful at stealing and derive great comfort and profit from it, though it be at someone else's expense.[20]

One kind of religious response to the phenomenological and epistemological challenge of culture is an abandonment of initiative, for it sets out to imitate empiricism and set up "laws and axioms" that are beyond dispute, using, or appearing to use, the rules of demonstration to sweep aside any basis for doubt.[21] That such a religious path is beset with difficulties is acknowledged when the proponents shift in the next stage to dealing with sin, for they propose as its remedy redemption through the emetic use of self-reproach. Religious subjectivism may be just as bereft of any ethical foundation as the secular force that feeds it, which is why instrumental mysticism, with its tendency toward self-moralization and psychic proofs, remains a problem for prophetic religion. It therefore follows that any sensible religious response must gather and nurture the numerous hints and clues in the language of progress and of the perfectibility of human institutions that Enlightenment thinkers and their successors employed, and bring them into convergence with the vision of a transcendent moral order. As John Oman has observed:

A higher morality is closely interwoven with a higher religion; and there is no form of religion in which there is not some beginning of a higher value for man and his society and some measure of better rule than impulse and better motive than fear or favour or any form of self-interest. [Even if we attend to his animal ancestry,] in man at any stage, the sense of the holy, however sunk in mere awe, the judgment of the sacred, however fettered in the material, and the sanction of the Supernatural, however beclouded by magic, make man's conduct in some sense moral, a standing above the mere

flux of impulse and circumstance, and an es-
timate of himself, his fellows and his ultimate
environment which is not measured by material
advantage (Oman 1931:388).

5

The Culture Crisis:
The Problem of Truth and Value

I said in the opening paragraph of this volume that my generation of undergraduates adopted the cultural project as the enlightened, rational alternative to religion — believing that we could advance the cause by the principles of cultural relativism and rejecting any reciprocity between cultures, because cultural reciprocity would open the door to cultural meddlesomeness, as with Christian missions. I want now to return to that theme and show how scientific positivism and the anthropology developing from it performed for us the functions of a religion, that is to say, an idealized construction of value-free cultural practices that we defended like sacred dogma against the obscurantist moralizations of religion.

In his penetrating inquiry into the history of anthropological science, David Bidney plotted the rise within the discipline of what he calls its natural science claims (Bidney 1953:682–99). Modern an-

thropologists made what to them was an important distinction by committing themselves to facts
and laws and leaving philosophers and humanists to
deal with values, a distinction that gained currency
only in the nineteenth century. By contrast, Renaissance thinkers believed in human perfectibility in
time, assuming that human beings could, under divine providence, perfect themselves and their institutions. There was general confidence of an inevitable
progress from primitiveness to civilization as from
darkness to light, with few limits set as to what
people could achieve in culture, in contrast to nature with its morally deficient, blind alleys. At that
stage both the optimist and the pessimist shared
the confidence in human instrumentality, the only
difference being that the optimist discounted any
possibility of regression whereas the pessimist felt
eternal vigilance was needed to prevent a slide into
the barbaric past.

The optimism that was characteristic of the
Renaissance was overthrown by an Enlightenment
cynicism that hardened into an antireligious stance,
placing religion, particularly the clerical maraboutic
forms of it, in the domain of the irrational and
obscurantist.[22] The most substantial division of
knowledge and reality in the Enlightenment formulations is the division between the progressive,
rational principles that conform to natural reason
and, on the other hand, unnatural, barbaric cus-

toms and conventions that conflict with natural reason. This was a major departure from the views of Renaissance thinkers who were not afraid to stake the entire enterprise on the issue of human perfectibility, with human beings performing a custodial responsibility under divine providence.

A further important shift occurred when, under the impact of scientific positivism, particularly that of Auguste Comte (1798–1857), modern anthropologists believed they could

> arrive at a knowledge of man's nature through a comparative study of culture history. Psychological laws were to be discovered as the final product of the study of comparative culture history, and they were not to be regarded as the presuppositions of historical study. Man was to be known through a study of culture history, not culture history through a study of man (Bidney 1953:684).

They conceived a progression from theology to metaphysics and finally to science that for Frazer was itself a phase still to be overtaken by an undefined stage. The next operational shift was to deduce the idea of God from effects in natural phenomena, that is to say, to make religion the illicit product of faulty reasoning. For these critics, religion constituted a logical false step in abstracting the notion of God from nature while imagining a real supernatural reality lurking in the shades. In this view the moral code is a function of geography, of cultural context. In the famous words of Pascal, "Three degrees of polar elevation overturn the whole system of jurisprudence. A meridian determines what is truth," so that, as someone else said, "somewhere east of Suez there ain't no ten commandments" (Pascal 1958).

The new Comtian advocates felt the real truth is that the laws of nature, being rational and progressive in the humanist sense, are more than adequate to take the place of divine providence. Thus, although appearing to keep an open mind about what might succeed science, scientific positivism was still dogmatic about excluding religion from any enlightened human dispensation.

Arthur Schlesinger, Jr., whose historical works we read in college, for example, could take it for granted that relativists have the truth on their side and that the advocates of the religious law have been the purveyors of darkness and death.[23] However, as a correspondent rightly noted, relativists are not as impeccable as they claim: the commandment "Thou shalt not kill," as an absolute rule, is a fundamental safeguard of life. "It's only when you add exceptions making it a relative prohibition that the slaughter begins" (Wilson 1989). In all its confident swagger this, then, was the reductionist relativism we inherited in our undergraduate education, kept alive by a cultural rage against moral universals or uniqueness, with cultural pluralism and relativity replacing earlier assertions about universal stages and types.

The position of Ruth Benedict, a student of Franz Boas, expresses very well the new attitude. She and her colleagues saw things differently. For them "historic cultures, whether literate or pre-literate, were regarded as aesthetic patterns or configurations, each of which is a legitimate expression of the potentialities of human nature. There is, it was held, no absolute normality or abnormality of social behavior; the abnormal is only that which is divergent from the cultural pattern of the community" (Bidney 1953:688).

Such a construction of the cultural project was, however, grounded in a specific liberal democratic cultural ethos and did not, therefore, abandon either the unilateralism of Enlightenment rationalists or the inductive principles of the positivists, a problem that dogged many cultural relativists. The problem came to a head during World War 2 when the United States War Department convened a special meeting of cultural anthropologists to get help in psychological campaigns against German National Socialism. One of these anthropologists objected to the purpose of the meeting on the grounds that scientific anthropology, being an objective discipline, carried no ethical biases as such and therefore could make no value judgments. "He went on to say that if the Germans preferred Nazism, they were entitled to that preference, just as democratic Americans are entitled to their own different preference," because "preference is simply an expression of [the] cultural milieu" in which we find it.[24]

A similar issue was involved when Melville Herskovits, a leading scholar of cultural anthropology, was confronted with the practical task of producing a charter of universal human rights for the United Nations. Herskovits adopts a concrete form of philosophical idealism and identifies himself with the statement of Cassirer that "experience is culturally defined" (Herskovits 1948:27), not just "conditioned." Herskovits continues: "Even the facts of the physical world are discerned through the enculturative screen so that the perception of time, distance, weight, size and other 'realities' is mediated by the conventions of any given group" (:63). For Herskovits there simply is no other reality than the social reality, and this absolute rule is the nemesis courting his theory of cultural relativism. Herskovits anticipates this criticism and says that our slowness or failure to concede the truth of cultural relativism is because we are bogged down in "the ethnocentric morass" of a puritanical religious culture. Yet such an outburst does not rescue his scheme; it merely repeats his denunciation of religion and appeals to us to propagate the prejudice.

At the behest of the executive board of the American Anthropological Association, Herskovits drafted a document on human rights for the United Nations in 1947. In the statement Herskovits made three salient points: (a) that individuals realize their potential only through culture, (b) that cultures are unique and different, with no valid scientific standard of objective evaluation, and (c) that standards of judgment are relative to the culture from which they derive. Consequently there can be no universal absolute moral codes, and therefore the attempt to impose a universal declaration of human rights on all mankind is scientifically invalid and morally indefensible (Bidney 1953:693). It must have been awkward for Herskovits to feel that his natural impulse to want to uphold certain liberal democratic codes for life and conduct and for maintaining standards of human decency against possible abuse by nondemocratic regimes must give way to "scientific" scruples of cultural noninterference.

The crux of the problem for cultural relativists is that in their concern to reject the unhealthy consequences of Western cultural and religious imperialism they reverted to a form of ethnocentrism in which other cultures are given license to be a law unto themselves and thus to be ethnocentric, with the stage set for proliferating plural cultural ethnocentrisms. The relativists have thus replaced the progressive ethnocentrism of the Enlightenment with their own serial ethnocentrism, with both sides retaining unilateral advantage and never really shaking free of historical particularity except, that is, by an illegitimate idealist route. It is hard to see how you could have cultural relativism without ethnocentrism. When Boas and Benedict, for instance, argue that the only scientific basis for intercultural harmony is mutual recognition of cultural equality and tolerance for difference (:688, 690), it is not entirely clear whether such a basis, laudable in itself, is "culturally determined," in which case its converse, of prejudice and intolerance, could conceivably also be "culturally determined," with no yardstick with which to adjudicate the matter. Nor is it clear how you could have unmitigated cultural relativism alongside any notion of absolute progress. Such would be the outcome of rigid adherence to "facts and laws."[25]

6

The Theological Issue

All of this leaves us with an acute problem in defining values. Full-blown cultural ethnocentrism is unacceptable because, relativists insist rightly, it encourages us to demean and devalue the cultures of others. Yet if our values are themselves culturally determined, then prejudice and domination, and ideas of "subjectivity" and "objectivity," cannot be judged except as "enculturative screens," and that simply will not do.

Cultural relativists have forced themselves into their own Procrustean bed by insisting that our choice is between a doctrine of fixed absolutes and one of historical cultural relativity, for in cultural determinism there is no logical connection between specific cultural facts and a general moral code, so that any meaningful choosing on our part is at best arbitrary, or else self-interested, but in either case a choosing that is a conditioned rather than an independent moral act. It still remains an issue that

human beings across cultures practice moral judgment and appeal to ethical rules, however diverse
and different the contexts, and if that were not the
case we would have blind conformity, aimless historical wandering, and worse. It would complicate
matters, with the relativist, for instance, robbed of
any virtue that might accrue to a worthy cause.

Unless a fresh term is introduced into the equation, we cannot escape the empirical dilemma of
cultural relativism, namely, how in pursuit of progressive values we can move from what *is* to what
ought to be. That "middle" term is not a "fact" we
can scoop up nor a "law" that belongs with ordering
the relationship of inanimate objects, but an intellectual lever that takes us somewhere different from
where it found us. That is how I would propose to
proceed: to recognize that the cultural project, in being spiritual and intellectual, is at heart a theological
matter, that reason is only secondarily human and
primarily divine, not the wear and tear of nature's ex-
terior drapery but its sap and fiber. Culture, "whether
personal or communal, is not reducible to genetics
or ethnicity because man is always capable of transcending his origins, that is, of ending his journey
in a different and better place than he began it"
(Levenson 1991:19).

Steiner's observation on the connection between
theology and modern cultural projects is appropriate
here, especially because it also deals with the issue of

Enlightenment rationalism and nineteenth-century logical positivism. Steiner argues that the special way in which we read a text today — comment, critique, and interpret it, derives directly from the study of Holy Scripture. He continues:

> Our grammars, our explications, our criticisms of texts, our endeavors to pass from letter to spirit, are the immediate heirs to the textualities of Western Judeo-Christian theology and biblical-patristic exegetics. What we have done since the masked scepticism of Spinoza, since the critiques of the rationalist Enlightenment and since the positivism of the nineteenth century, is to borrow vital currency, vital investments and contracts of trust from the bank or treasure-house of theology. It is from there that we have borrowed our theories of the symbol, our use of the iconic, our idiom of poetic creation and aura. It is loans of terminology and reference from the reserves of theology which provide the master readers in our time (such as Walter Benjamin and Martin Heidegger) with their license to practice. We have borrowed, traded upon, made small change of the reserves of transcendent authority (Steiner 1986:20).

Steiner calls the misuse of religion by our secular, agnostic civilization an "embarrassed act of larceny," involving as it does the act of drawing from a source while loudly trumpeting its bankruptcy, or, in the subject I now want to treat, robbing the religious metaphysic to service a political metaphysic, for that is how the modern national state has emerged in Western consciousness. Thus, in his penetrating analysis of the state as the symbol of "the life-energy of the European race," Troeltsch shows the serious moral deficiencies of cultural ethnocentrism expressed in political institutions, including the state.

The ethnocentric state elevates military science and bureaucratic rules to a transcendent ethic, giving directions and goals in human affairs an absolute normative status. Troeltsch says that we must be able to live as human beings, which might become the legitimate subject of the state, but that we live not for the sake of mere physical existence but for the sake of ideas and ideals from which the state derives its ultimate meaning and value. He insists that the state as the possessor and user of power ought to come under the authority of what he termed "the indestructible moral idea" (Troeltsch 1991).[26] Troeltsch goes on to argue that the separation of state and culture has allowed the state to push aside higher culture or otherwise harness it to its own interests, whereas higher culture for its part, sundered from a political ethic, is inclined to become escapist, the society of Orphic initiates.

Nationalism often acts to fuse the otherwise separate impulses of culture and politics, and by its force produces a sentiment indistinguishable from the religious. Nationalism offers people a creed every bit as potent as religion, with love and devotion to one's people and country a competitor in the altruistic sense with faith in God and the hereafter. Honor and duty thus arise from citizenship nearly as faithfulness and submission arise from religious faith, for both prove their claims from the personal sacrifices individuals are constrained to make.

Nationalism in this understanding effectively combines persuasion with sanction, self-denial with personal vindication, natural ties with acquired skills, the struggle for existence with giving one's life, and so on. "By thus identifying oneself with the state, one no longer needs to fear any superior power, except possibly God; in this sense of inviolability, one experiences a value that transcends egoism because it [i.e., the value] relates not to the individual but to the whole, and is made possible by an intense self-discipline and personal subjection" (:179). The state in these circumstances would come to regard "itself as a source of ethical value and moral obligation. It can (and often does) invest this claim with all the pathos of moral sentiment" (:179). Yet, as Troeltsch admits, nationalism that is thus sacralized and absolutized becomes a source of the demonic and the depraved, in Europe and elsewhere, including programs of "ethnic cleansing."

Taking up a similar theme, the American philosopher William Ernest Hocking identifies the grounds for a limited theory of state sovereignty, saying that the state furnishes the conditions under which people can make themselves. The state, he argues, is necessary to enable rational planning to take place, including planning for the future. However, this future planning function of the state, Hocking says, is perceived as representing "man's longer will" and is consequently given an objective status, leading to the wrong conclusion that the state is capable of civilizing human beings, of leading us out of ignorance and stagnation into knowledge of the future and progress.

Hocking spoke confidently of the state as political community having its counterpart in the religious community that embraces the "totality of the ultimate state of man, representing a dimension which the state cannot reach" (Hocking 1956:2). The state, in Hocking's view, does not speak for the cosmos but for a community of people limited in scope and wisdom. In spite of that, he says, the expectation has grown of the state's superior right to conceive and speak for the attainable good life, leading to the view that it is the church, not the state, that will in time wither away. This, Hocking insists, is the secular hypothesis: the state will satisfy human nature and succeed in its work. Yet, Hocking cautions, the state is inadequate in itself; it "depends for its vitality upon a [spiritual] motivation which it cannot by itself command" (:6).

The religious case against the doctrinaire state is a solid one, because "religion is the affirmation of the anchorage in reality of ideal ends" (:30). The very nature of the secular, pragmatic state is that it is a human, finite contrivance, "and the gap between the finite and the infinite remains — infinite. If...it is with the infinite that we have always to do, the state must be infinitely short of complete competence" (:44). In which case, the state's finite capacity would turn oppressive once it assumes the prerogatives of the infinite. "A strong State without a strong Church, as recent events have vividly shown, will inevitably assume some, and perhaps most, of the attributes of unchecked absolutism" (Grubb 1947).

A most trenchant question under these circumstances is whether it is meaningful to speak of the separation of creed and culture when the distinction is effaced in a state-cultural transposition. Gellner describes such a situation when he refers to the transition "from faith to culture, to its fusion with ethnicity and eventually with a state." Institutional religion, in becoming reverent retailer of cultural conventions, often acts accordingly to place a premium on ethnic identity. Consequently, "high religions [are] those which are fortified by a script and sustained by specialized personnel, which some-

times, though by no means always, become the basis
of a new collective identity in the industrial world,
making the transition, so to speak, from a culture-
religion to a culture-state." He illustrates this with
the example of a character in Anton Chekhov's *Three
Sisters,* as follows: "Perhaps you think this German is
getting over-excited. But on my word of honour, I'm
Russian. I cannot even speak German. My father is
Orthodox" (Gellner 1983:72).

This situation, however common, represents the
failure and collapse of the moral vision, as is well expressed by George Santayana's quip that "our nation-
ality is like our relations to women: too implicated in
our moral nature to be changed honourably, and too
accidental to be worth changing" (cited in Gellner
1983: x). On that view, national or ethnic exclusive-
ness is a force whose power, whether tamed or not,
entangles our being — a grim, if true, account of the
consequences of ethno-cultural moralization.

Thus, when Aristotle reflected critically on what
might be involved in transcending our natural limitations and thus securing our felicity as human beings,
he did the best he could in the circumstances and left
the door open to a theological inquiry. He suggested
that we aspire to the fount itself and not be content
with the mere trickle of the natural order.[27]

If happiness is activity in accordance with
virtue, it is reasonable that it should be in ac-

cordance with the highest virtue; and this will be the best thing in us. Whether it be reason or something else that is this element which is thought to be our natural ruler and guide and to take thought of things noble and divine, whether it be itself also divine or only the most divine element in us, the activity of this in accordance with its proper virtue will be perfect happiness (*Nicomachean Ethics*, Bk X, Ch 7).

The comment of C. S. Lewis that "when we are forced to admit that reason cannot be merely human, there is no longer any compulsive inducement to say that virtue is purely human" articulates an insight that returns the arc to its point of maximum tension, marking a fitting consummation of Aristotle's design.[28]

Similarly, when Bacon writes of God's book and God's works as two necessary sources of knowledge, he allows the view that the pen as reason is mightier than the spade and higher than "centaurs and chimeras," the gods of whim and fancy. We should see that "human reason in the act of knowing is illuminated by the Divine reason" (Lewis 1963:26–27). This is so because reason in that sense has to break free sufficiently from the chain of causation to be at the behest of what it knows. It is the characteristic of the knower as subject that, as al-Ghazali (1054–

1111) would express it with reference to religion, the believer's "heart has reasons his reason does not know" (Averroës 1954:vol 1).

Thus the chain of causation in which we lock up all of nature turns out to have a key in the insight of reason; it is that insight that gave us by inference the chain in the first place. As Chesterton remarked concerning the pervasive anti-Aristotelian material determinism of our day, it is absurd to claim that people are rational and objective because they come to no conclusion, and that religion is subjective and untrustworthy for bringing us to conclusions. Such a claim, Chesterton points out, is based on "the quite unproved proposition of the independence of matter and quite improbable proposition of its power to originate mind" (Chesterton 1969:137).[29] There is a certain tautology such unexamined assumptions produce, such as that no intelligent person would believe in religion, and therefore intelligent persons who do (such as Pasteur, Newton, Faraday, Einstein, or Newman) cease to count as such, or, as Chesterton puts it, "first you challenge me to produce a black swan, and when I produce a score you rule them all out because they were black" (1969:138). Yet the conclusion to which religion would bring us presses hard even on our resistance, namely, the awesome grandeur of Cosmic Reason as our Creator and Maker. Lewis puts it as follows:

In so far as thought is merely human, merely a characteristic of one particular biological species, it does not explain our knowledge. Where thought is strictly rational it must be in some odd sense, not ours, but cosmic or super-cosmic. It must be something not shut up inside our heads but already "out there" — in the universe or behind the universe: either as objective as material Nature, or more objective still. Unless all that we take to be knowledge is an illusion, we must hold that in thinking we are not reading rationality into an irrational universe but responding to a rationality with which the universe has always been saturated (Lewis 1967:65).[30]

In the final analysis, the religious view that creation has a purpose and that we as human beings hold it in moral stewardship may be decisive for any enlightened cultural project, in the same way that the inflexibility of both the right-wing romantic "return to nature" and the left-wing ideological reductionism could be its ruin. This would explain why even the imaginative synthesizing of an exalted reason and an idealized beauty to create an aesthetic harmony appears to have failed because both reason and beauty were torn from their common moral framework, so that Voltaire's "cultivated garden" (*il faut cultiver notre jardin*) seemed as much like the valley of dead bones as Montaigne's dry cynicism (*il nous faut abestir pour nous assagir*). Retreat in the one instance is answered by defiance in the other, and in both cases we have merely *homo mensura* ("man as the measure of all things") as first and last resort. Lessing tried to make a virtue of this sense of forlorn heroism in the following words:

> If God were to hold in His right hand all truth, and in His left the single, ever-living impulse to seek for truth, though coupled with the condition of eternal error, and should say to me, "Choose!" I would humbly fall before His left hand, and say, "Father, give! Pure truth is, after all, for Thee alone (Rolleston 1889: 201).

This kind of heroism belongs not with the nature of the facts as we know them but with the moral sense that transcends nature. We may recall the words of John Stuart Mill that all the things for which human beings are hanged or imprisoned for doing are routinely committed by nature, including "hundreds of hideous deaths" that surpass the cruelty of a Domitian. "All this," Mill pleads, "Nature does with the most supercilious disregard both of mercy and of justice" (1958). Such a plea appeals to the tribunal of our heart and brings us up against the moral grain. A line in the liturgy of the East Syrian Church expresses the sentiment well when it affirms:

"Thou hast clothed us with a moral nature which our trespasses ever painfully oppress."

The quest for the cultural ideal, then, contains this melancholy strain, defying us to set a course that would not eventually rejoin the main tributary in which all streams renew themselves by discharging their moral tribute. Some of that impulse still stirs in the depths even of apparent indifference and other forms of moral sluggishness, the thin blue line that separates us from the nature of Mill's description. And it is precisely this that makes religion, even religion in its deterrent form, in what it repudiates, qualitatively different from rational defiance or self-indulgence in which the enterprise can be no greater or higher than what would be at stake in a heroic self-vindication, as in Wagner's Wotan.

There is a real qualitative, moral change involved in the religious life, because "[t]he moment that some things are sacred, man has begun to live in the world which provides for him the substance and the sanction of his ideals: and the change appears as much in the quality of his disloyalty to them as of his faithfulness" (Oman 1931:388–89). It is reasonable to infer from the mother tongue appropriation of Christianity that indigenous ideals received such a reinforcement, thus mitigating distortions that occurred in other spheres.

7

Religion and the Mother Tongue: A Postlude

If the whole Western enterprise consists in nothing other than heroic exploits of self-assertion, then of course the historical facts of the Western encounter with other cultures and societies could with justice be read as unequivocal facts of violence and domination. If, on the other hand, Western Christianity, though sharing in all the cultural forms of the larger society, was nevertheless not ultimately synonymous with those forms, then Christianity in its locally appropriated forms would introduce some ambiguity into cultural encounter, such that there would be ambivalence, paradox, and other unintended consequences resulting from the encounter. This would not deny the real destruction and harm that accompanied Western expansion abroad, including missionary denigration of non-Western cultures. It says something for Christianity as a cultural captive of the West that missionaries should more often than not be agitated by cultural differences and seldom excited by genuine religious similarities, so religiously tone deaf had they become in their own culture.

The question we must examine, however briefly, is whether the Western cultural project is so flawed that contact with other cultures imperils those cultures to the same extent. Modern historical examples of the West's violent intrusion into other societies do not, on the face of it, encourage a different conclusion, and it would be disingenuous in the extreme to pretend otherwise. Yet, unless we were to adopt a rather extreme view of comprehensive indigenous defeat, it seems reasonable to think that some pockets of resistance remained within which local initiatives could prosper and bear fruit, with or without Western encouragement. If that were the case, it would make Western cultural contact one factor, albeit a fundamental factor, in the total historical picture whose focus might now be local interlocutors and the agency role they assumed as translators, interpreters, vade mecums, colporteurs, teachers, writers, preachers, catechists, secretaries, and so on — not an insignificant shift of emphasis, for it shows cultural encounter to have had on that level a positive effect.

It is a fact of no trivial import that such local agents played a pivotal role in their societies and were preponderant in numerous places well before the West had politically and economically asserted its undisputed overlordship. These agents carried forward the impulse for local awakening amidst all the ambiguities of alien rule. Their history, and that of the colonized societies of which they were a part, is a standing reminder of the unintended and ramifying consequences of mother tongue development, and, in particular, of how indigenous cultural values survived the otherwise withering effects of Western technological superiority.

Religion provides a reliable clue into what is involved in the cultural reappraisal we are urging here. In their encounter with the West, for example, Africans were conscious that the West intended not merely to intimidate and control, for that would involve a disproportionate use of scarce resources to keep down a sullen people. Such a course of action, Africans recognized, might produce respect, even awe, for the West, but not trust and loyalty. So Africans saw that if their encounter with the West had any meaning and depth to it, then both sides would have to do a fundamental mutual reckoning in terms of truth, justice, integrity, and the hopes of a common humanity — in other words, those matters that pertain to the imperishable treasures of the human spirit, that is, religion. As it was, in several instances both Africans and the colonial administrators conceded the affinity of creed and culture by each side seeking to enlist missionaries — Africans because

religion was inseparable from personal and community life, and administrators because even if church
and state were separated by constitutional fiat, state-
craft of the imperialistic variety needed a metaphysic
of white superiority, one that missions might ide-
ally provide. Thus, in their tacit agreement to look
to missions for support, administrators and nationals, often unbeknown to each other, advanced their
separate causes from a common source, with the advantage going to the nationals who were empowered
from mother tongue agency.

It is impossible that missionaries should devote
so much time and effort to mother tongues without
being aware at some point or other of the wider
consequences of what they were doing, and the
evidence is that many were conscious of that. Indeed, the vernacular Scriptures missions pioneered
in the field converged with indigenous aspirations
to bring missionaries to a sympathetic espousal of
local cultures. Thus we may refer to the work of
Johannes Christaller in Ghana, to that of the American Board of Commissioners for Foreign Mission in
South Africa, to the story of Bishop John Colenso
of Cape Town and his African and European colleagues, to the importance of David Livingstone
and his reflections on the mother tongue. These
and many other examples provide evidence of fresh
combinations and permutations in narrative creativity, in particular, examples of where the written

form gave narrative materials an extended popular appeal.

The religious foundations of African narrative discourse received an unprecedented boost with the vernacular Scriptures. Africans found in the many great stories of the Bible, including the parables of Jesus with their homely, down-to-earth figures, a sublime evocation of the oral culture that in traditions were handed down from mouth to mouth and recounted in family and community settings. Consequently, the vernacular Scriptures came as the ringing assurance of voices people knew and trusted. We may thus imagine how the Bible in the mother tongue would become what Oliver Wendell Holmes calls "the shrine of the people's soul." So many disparate groups and communities, with nothing else in common, found themselves in the same company only from being able to recognize something of themselves in the characters and personages of Scripture — the great figures of the Old and New Testaments: Abraham, Moses, Samuel, David, Elijah, Sarah, Leah, Ruth, Naomi, Elizabeth, and Mary; the sites of God's encounter: Mamre, Sinai, the Red Sea, Bethel, and Bethlehem — all transformed in the peculiar indigenous crucible. It was as if Samuel and Elijah and Isaiah spoke in the people's idiom and in the cadences of the exalted ancestors. Thus could Johannes Christaller, the great missionary-linguist, urge Africans, especially Christian Africans, "not to despise the sparks of truth entrusted to and preserved by their own people, and let them not forget that by entering into their way of thinking and by acknowledging what is good and expounding what is wrong they will gain the more access to the hearts and minds of their less favoured countrymen" (Christaller, cited in Danquah 1944:186). Thus, too, could Edwin Smith inveigh against foisting an artificial culture on Africans, for the African "cannot be treated as if he were a European who happened to be born black. He ought not to be regarded as if he were a building so badly constructed that it must be torn down, its foundations torn up and a new structure erected on its site, on a totally new plan and with entirely new materials" (Smith 1926:295).

On the issue of colonial authorities imposing European languages like English, Smith was cogent, saying, "to insist upon an African abandoning his own tongue and to speak and think in a language so different as English, is like demanding that the various Italian peoples should learn Chinese in order to overcome their linguistic problem" (Smith 1926: 303). Professor Diedrich Westermann of Berlin and a former missionary to Africa appealed for mother tongue literacy. "If the African is to keep and develop his own soul and is to become a separate personality, his education must not begin by inoculating him with a foreign civilization, but it must implant respect for the indigenous racial life, it must teach him to love his country and tribe as gifts given by God which are to be purified and brought to full growth by the new divine life. One of these gifts," he continues, "is the vernacular, it is the vessel in which the whole national life is contained and through which it finds expression" (Westermann 1925:28). Both Westermann and Edwin Smith knew of the contrary policy adopted for India by Alexander Duff, and they were determined that there would be no repeating of that in Africa.

Nor, for that matter, did the history of the northern peoples of Europe and North America entirely support Duff in the Indian case. Walt Whitman, in his *November Boughs,* spoke for his and other generations when he affirmed: "I've said nothing yet of the Bible as a poetic entity, and of every portion of it. . . . How many ages and generations have brooded and wept and agonized over this book! . . . Translated in all languages, how it has united the diverse world! Not only does it bring us what is clasped within its covers. Of its thousands there is not a verse, not a word, but is thick-studded with human emotion" (Whitman 1982:1141–42), human emotion that is the fuel of artistic and cultural creativity. And thus did critics credit Tyndale with having "created the glories of English prose" in his translation of the Bible: "Though I speak with the tongues of men and of angels, and have not charity, I am

become as sounding brass, or a tinkling cymbal."
Such are the common, homely figures Tyndale employed that have survived as pearls in many of our
versions.

It is hard to imagine the scandal this caused to the
cultural proprietors of the day. Sir Arthur Quiller-
Couch, in his Cambridge lectures on the subject,
reminded us that the idioms we assume to be original are not in fact so. Isaiah did not, he challenged,
write the cadences of his prophecies as we know
them; Christ did not speak the cadences of the parables or the Sermon on the Mount as we know them.
"These have been supplied by the translators. By all
means let us study them and learn to delight in them;
but Christ did not suffer for the cadences invented
by Englishmen almost 1600 years later" (1920:137).
And then, drawn by the power that joined majestic
transcendence to exalted condescension and fixed it
in Tyndale's vicarious suffering, Quiller-Couch concluded that our translated Bible haunts and moves
us because "it is everything we see, hear, feel, because it is in us, in our blood" (:156). You could
not put the truth of cultural origin and practice
into truer, more succinct, and more intimate words.
The biographer of the Jesuit missionary to India,
Robert de Nobili, takes up this theme of cultural
intimacy, and spoke of de Nobili's commitment in
that regard, saying de Nobili "was aware that no
amount of learning could replace the deepest springs

within the soul, fed by blood, tradition and climate, and crystallized in a mother tongue" (Cronin 1959:173).

It is necessary to recall at this stage the divergence of mother tongue development from the Enlightenment where cultural ideas were influenced by the theory of universal paradigms, with contingent facts treated as episodes of deep underlying structures of unity in the name of which cultural and linguistic diversity was construed as an obstacle, and was thus discounted. The study of languages and cultures in this Enlightenment scheme was essentially the study of a universal theory and grammar, with the consequence of linguistic and cultural variety being held hostage to an idealized conceit. Winckelmann was speaking from this tradition. The modern linguistic work of missions, by contrast, promoted extraordinary variety, with languages being treated as internally coherent systems whose essential spark would be preserved in the process and outcome of translating the Scriptures. This came quite close to our ideas of cultural relativism, with the difference that by retaining the notion of a higher purpose subsisting in the enterprise, the agents of this transformation assumed local cultures to have the inherent capacity for change, and thus salvaged local history from the moribund, ethnocentric fate of cultural relativists. In this instance, faith in God as personal savior invested the pre-Christian dispensation with its own self-consistent original *telos*. Eventually, however circuitous or checkered the route, this commenced an immense theological inquiry that became the intellectual foundation for personal commitment, cultural renewal, and public responsibility.

Thus, when we assess whether Western contact has had a harmful or beneficial effect on non-Western populations, whether, to take even more specific forms of the question, modern Western Christian missions in Africa have damaged or advanced local cultural practices and aspirations, we emerge with a rather complex understanding, one that throws new light on the question of whether culture contact can be completely innocent and neutral, in which case so-called "contact" is a misnomer, or whether, as I have argued, contact can be mutually beneficial as well as harmful. The proponents of innocent culture contact deny its possibility and thus invoke the harmful alternative. That view is what has carried the main charge of expounding and explaining the work of Christian missions, including the process of religious conversion, in Africa and elsewhere. Yet, even if we are reluctant to abandon the victim view of non-Western populations, we may still acknowledge the long-dormant frontiers of creativity that have consequently been opened up by mother tongue development, frontiers that cultures must cross to transcend themselves. The material aspects of such culture change are easy enough to describe, thanks to the thriving industry of postcolonial economic development theory.

What is equally obvious, though harder to accept, is that material progress has its internal personal counterpart. Change in our outward circumstances would be arid without a sense of solidarity with the spirit that calls us into the future. Historical progress lies not in acquiescence, whether to Western domination or to ethnic ideologies of primordial innocence, but in the self-striving that attempts to apply the imperative of personal transformation to the conditions of lived experience, just as the candle, in consuming its store, radiates light. A similar paradox should be seen in the way mother tongue development sparked the native cultural impulse to usher in immense movements of renewal and rehabilitation, whatever the incidence of friction and intolerance vis-à-vis the West. Scriptural translation into the mother tongue consecrates what is wholesome; and, where there is genuine ethical response, it also attenuates intertribal malice. In any case, such translation brings into the foreground latent possibilities as well as any endemic tensions, and, through the scriptural norms of salvific truth and the language of neighborliness, traditional communities may transcend their own ethnocentric limitations. In this sense, then, we confront the issue of creed and culture in their positive combination. In the unstable conditions of traditional cultures reeling from the collision with modernity, it is easy to see how culture can be fomented with messianic fervor to produce the kind of political monism by which ethnic insecurity tries to immunize itself against the feared virus of global exposure. Having the Scriptures in the mother tongue helps to mitigate those tendencies, or at any rate to offer an alternative vision. Some such outcome is profoundly congruous with the religious stake in the demands for global neighborliness, suggesting how world Christianity might contain the promise of the new humanity for the twenty-first century and beyond.

Notes

1. It is my contention that the translation of the Bible into indigenous languages constituted a tacit surrender to indigenous primacy and complicates the arguments of Western superiority. Whatever linguistic distortions, compromises, egregious inventions, and other forms of invasive interference missionaries may have introduced, the shift into the vernacular paradigm, in the long run if not immediately, would excite local ambition and fuel national feeling.

2. Many modern cultural projects have set themselves the task of fighting religion as antirational and have found it hard not to become the shadow image of the enemy. Voltaire (1694–1778), for instance, exploited historical examples to attack religion, but distorted presixteenth-century Christianity through his peculiar telescoping of history. Collingwood points out gaps of this kind in Voltaire's historical method and draws attention to its cramping effect on his view of religion. He notes how the historical school founded by Voltaire took little interest in the remoter past or, we might add, in non-Western societies (Collingwood 1984:246–47). Such omissions have left their mark on both Kant (1724–1804) and Hume (1711–76), as also on the pop avatars of the 1960s and their perfunctory view of culture history. For them knowledge was like a biological organism, a complex pattern and combination of feelings rooted in sensation and emotion — feelings that by their nature are specifically conditioned by Western culture (Bury 1913:113).

3. For an assessment of these writers, see Edward Evans-Pritchard, *A History of Anthropological Thought*, ed. André Singer (New York: Basic Books, 1981), and Evans-Pritchard, *Theories of Primitive Religion* (Oxford: Clarendon Press, 1962).

4. For an exhaustive historical treatment of the subject, see Keith Thomas, *Religion and the Decline of Magic* (New York: Charles Scribner's Sons, 1971).

5. Even when he meant to be damning, Pliny wrote that magic "embraces the three acts that most rule the human mind, medicine, religion and mathematics — a triple chain that enslaves mankind" (Glover 1975:18).

6. Bacon elaborated on this, saying he understood magic "in general as the science which applies the knowledge of hidden forms to the production of wonderful operations" (Wightman 1972:142–43).

7. For aspects of this subject, see Gilbert Ryle, *The Concept of Mind* (London: Hutchinson & Co., 1949; repr. Penguin Books, 1990).

8. The words are those of Paracelsus. See "The Paracelsian Movement" in Hugh Trevor-Roper, *Renaissance Essays* (Chicago: University of Chicago Press, 1985), 49–99.

9. In *The New Atlantis* Bacon wrote: "The end of our foundation is the knowledge of causes and the secret motion of things and the enlarging of the bounds of human empire, so the effecting of all things possible." See also Medawar (1969).

10. This view came into ascendancy in the Enlightenment and has its roots in classical Greek sources. As we will see at the end of this volume, Aristotle, for one, promotes the virtue of "moderation" as an expression of contemplative mental exercise (*Nicomachean Ethics,* Bk X, Ch 7). The two fundamental principles of culture considered under this intellectual legacy were defined as the idea of humanity and of progress or of teleology as in Aristotle, in contrast to the activist and exploitative employment of human powers. Bacon, who might be considered the founder of culture in the modern sense, wrote in his *Advancement of Learning* (1605) that the day on which God rested at creation was deemed more blessed than the other six on which he labored, whereas from the records of antiquity we learn that founders of states were but demigods and inventors among the gods themselves. For Bacon the life of contemplation was far superior to the life of conquest, which makes culture a matter of culture-consciousness and thus of progress toward hu-

manistic consciousness. It is an idea permeating all modern theories of culture.

11. George Steiner assesses Kant's long-range impact in this area as decisive. He says: "The logical and psychological location by Kant of fundamental perceptions within human reason, Kant's conviction that the 'thing in itself,' the ultimate reality-substance out there, could not be analytically defined or demonstrated, let alone articulated, laid the ground for solipsism and doubt. A dislocation of language from reality, of designation from perception, is alien to Kant's idealism of common sense; but it is an important potential" (Steiner 1986:2). See also Geoffrey H. Hartman, "Art and Consensus in the Era of Progressive Politics," *The Yale Review,* 80, no. 4 (1992): 50–61.

12. A modern philosopher traces a similar epistemology to Hegel, saying Kierkegaard, for example, found the root of the problem "in the philosophy of Hegel, according to which the historical particulars became subsumed under the generalizing abstractions of reason.... Particularity was lost in abstraction, the individual person in the mass of society. Hegel was himself rooted in the Enlightenment, which in turn rested on the terms of Greek rationalism that the Enlightenment developed in its own peculiar way" (Gunton 1992:84).

13. Thus Schiller praised naiveté as the mark of natural genius, a view that allowed him to classify literary and poetic genius according to how the subject of human alienation from nature is treated. "The poet," he declared, "either *is* nature or he *seeks* her. One makes a naive poet, the other a sentimental one" (*Über naive und sentimentalische Dichtung,* 1796). Naive poets apprehend the truth of nature immediately, whereas sentimental ones pick their way by hints and clues that are for the moment unbundled.

14. Max Stirner, *The Ego and His Own,* 1845; Turgenieff, *Fathers and Children,* 1861; Ibsen's writings, in particular *Brand,* 1865, *Peer Gynt,* 1867, and *Emperor and Galilean,* 1873, and Edvard Grieg's musical settings of some of Ibsen's works; Emerson, *The American Scholar,* 1837.

15. Goethe's solution in *Faust* to claim "activity" as a function of "nostalgia," and therefore as a principle of consciousness, returns to

the problem by a different route, extrapolating from a mode of necessary cultural activity remedies for a transcendent moral condition. In the final analysis, the Goethean project depends for its success on the passionate egoist joining forces with the thinking egoist: "Verweile doch, du bist so schön." All of which recalls Plato (in the *Republic*) considering poetry and drama as parasitic and consequently banishing them from the state. The "culture problem" is not, however, simply a matter of arguing for what is necessary and useful, but of conceiving the human enterprise in such terms as are compatible with our overwhelming sense of moral truth.

16. Soon after the war was concluded, the pope promptly sent as his apostolic representative a notorious Fascist and replaced with Italians all non-Italian Catholic missionaries in the country, not excepting a French bishop who had spent fifty years in the country.

17. John Carey has written about the unwarranted sense of moral superiority that characterized, for example, the British and Irish intellectual class whose views on cultural breeding targeted the lower social classes as fit for extermination (Carey 1992). Paul Johnson remarked in his review, "Faithful Christians and orthodox Jews are about the only groups who can be relied on to provide tough opposition" to such ideas (Johnson 1992).

18. Freud asserts that cultural ideals and the achievement that fostered them are of a narcissistic nature, giving pride and satisfaction to members, though nationalism also foments discord and enmity (Freud 1975). If this is so, then we are left with cultural confusion as an endemic and ultimately a destructive force.

19. My own brother was adopted thus by a childless maternal relative.

20. Freud observes in this regard: "There are countless civilized people who would shrink from murder or incest but who do not deny themselves the satisfaction of their avarice, their aggressive urges or their sexual lusts, and who do not hesitate to injure other people by lies, fraud and calumny, so long as they remain unpunished for it" (1961:12). Fear in those circumstances would be based on an apprehension of a prescriptive code.

21. It is relevant to consider how Bertrand Russell, for one, took up the issue of mathematical certainty, thinking it might of-

fer knowledge that was "indubitable," only to abandon it "after some twenty years of very arduous toil" because "if certainty were indeed discoverable in mathematics, it would be in a new kind of mathematics" (1975:725). The attempt at a comparable kind of risk-free knowledge in religion is destined to fare no better. Newman sees the issue differently, saying "there is no ultimate test of truth besides the testimony born to truth by the mind itself" (Ker 1990:618–50, 646).

22. The work of Edward Gibbon (1737–94), as has been pointed out by many writers, fits into this combative mold, and its historical roots reach back to the Republican morality of the French Revolution in which the ideas of Socrates, Marcus Aurelius, and Cicero were declared the new religion of deism known as Theophilanthropy. Its advocates intended it to replace the refurbished Christianity of Rousseau. Its doctrines were God, humanity, fraternity, and immortality. Napoleon in 1801 ended the brief reign of this religion, when the state adopted a contrived amalgam of Rousseau and Christian idealism. However, its ideas maintained a hold on the intellectual elites, so that, even as late as 1905, when the church-state Concordat came to an end, the antireligious rationalism eventually reasserted itself.

23. Arthur Schlesinger, Jr., "The Opening of the American Mind," *The New York Times Book Review*, July 23, 1989. Schlesinger used strong terms to put down religion, accusing it of intolerance, bigotry, and self-centeredness. But it is well to remember that he cites with approval Reinhold Niebuhr's neo-Calvinist morality as essential for de-absolutizing secular and mundane structures, and the human instrument as finite and provisional vis-à-vis God's absolute and universal purpose. Niebuhr's central conviction about human power and institutions being always precarious and fragmentary is, says Schlesinger, indispensable to democratic values and historical realism. In fact, Niebuhr's position can be traced back to the Reformers and, before them, to Pauline theology, pioneers of the "absolutism" Schlesinger otherwise pillories.

24. Reported by James Luther Adams in his Introduction to Troeltsch's *The Absoluteness of Christianity and the History of Religion* (1971:7). Robert Redfield, a cultural anthropologist and a participant at the meeting, tried, however, to split the issue, on

the one hand, between scientific objectivity and its determinist ethical, or nonethical, consequences, and, on the other, the actions of free and moral human agents. Redfield's solution aggravates, rather than resolves, the problem, because if cultural relativism disqualifies moral judgment by its superior objective scientific method, then moral judgment is spurious and as such inferior, and vulnerable, to demonstrable objective facts.

25. Troeltsch observes in this connection: "The doctrine of endless progress, or rather the theory of endless change, is a groundless prejudgment that seems plausible only to people who have consigned all metaphysical ideas regarding a transcendent background of history to the status of an illusion — and with such ideas the religious belief in the unity and meaningfulness of reality" (1971:94).

26. Troeltsch was born in 1865 and died in 1923.

27. Aristotle held that intellectual inquiry and the ordinary life of civic virtue would indeed harmonize by a natural teleological development, but he misses the cultural factors that might warp such a process.

28. Lewis's statement may be read not as seeking to rescue Aristotle's teleology but as concerning itself with the nature of thought as such.

29. In his essay "The American Scholar," Emerson writes confidently of nature as mental life, so that "in the mass and in particle, Nature hastens to render account of herself to the mind" (1960:65). Compare that view to that of John Stuart Mill, who wrote: "The appearances in nature forcibly suggest the idea of a maker (or makers), and therefore all mankind have believed in gods," although Mill goes on to say that these appearances also contradict the idea of a perfectly good maker (1988: 659).

30. This view of the universe stands right at the heart of Christian theology, in contrast to the timeless notions of philosophical idealism. This timeless view of nature is analogous to the view of nature as necessary, rather than only as contingent. It is as such that Emerson, for example, would want to promote Nature in the upper case. "The astronomer discovers that geometry, a pure abstraction of the human mind, is the measure of planetary motion. The chemist finds proportion and intelligible method throughout matter; and sci-

ence is nothing but the finding of analogy, identity, in the most remote parts. The ambitious soul will sit down before each refractory fact; one after another reduces all strange constitutions, all new powers, to their class and their law, and goes on forever to animate the last fiber of organization, the outskirts of nature, by insight. Thus to him, to this schoolboy under the bending dome of day, is suggested that he and it proceed from one root; one is leaf and one is flower, relation, sympathy, stirring in every vein" (Emerson 1960:66). To that extent Emerson has jettisoned any notion of the historical character of the world, finding truth in the "inner life, a life stripped of the past because it was conceived by a regenerate soul in nature" (Barish 1989:174), as his biographer says. Bertrand Russell (1872–1970) rejects this Hegelian monism, saying it collapses everything into the subject-predicate form (Russell 1975:674). It is, however, difficult to reconcile Russell's own high ethical idealism with his strong hedonism, his complaint against all that makes "a mockery of what human life should be" with his call for passionate expressive fulfillment.

References Cited

Averroës. 1954. *The Incoherence of the Incoherence.* Ed. and trans. Simon den Bergh. London: Luzac & Co.

Barish, Evelyn. 1989. *Emerson: The Roots of Prophecy.* Princeton: Princeton University Press.

Bidney, David. 1953. The Concept of Value in Modern Anthropology. In *Anthropology Today: An Encyclopedic Inventory.* Chicago: University of Chicago Press. Pp. 682–99.

Bury, J. B. 1913. *A History of Freedom of Thought.* New York: Henry Holt & Co.

Carey, John. 1992. *The Intellectuals and the Masses: Pride and Prejudice Among the Literary Intelligentsia 1880–1938.* London: Faber & Faber.

Chesterton, G. K. 1969. *All Things Considered.* Philadelphia: Dufour Editions. First published 1908.

Collingwood, R. G. 1984. *An Essay on Metaphysics.* Lanham, Md.: University Press of America. First published in 1939 by Oxford University Press.

Cronin, Vincent. 1959. *A Pearl to India: The Life of Robert de Nobili.* London: Rupert Hart Davis.

Danquah, J. B. 1944. *The Akan Doctrine of God.* London: Lutterworth Press.

Emerson, Ralph Waldo. 1960. *Selections from Ralph Waldo Emerson.* Ed. Stephen E. Whicher. Boston: Houghton Mifflin.

Evans-Pritchard, Edward E. 1962. *Theories of Primitive Religion.* Oxford: Clarendon Press.

———. 1981. Study of Frazer and Levy-Bruhl, in André Singer, ed.

Freud, Sigmund. 1961. *The Future of an Illusion.* Ed. and trans. James Strachey. New York: W. W. Norton.

Gellner, Ernest. 1983. *Nations and Nationalism.* Ithaca: Cornell University Press. First published 1983.

Gillman, Peter, and Leni Gillman. 1980. *Collar the Lot! How Britain Intervened and Expelled Wartime Refugees.* London and New York: Quartet Books.

Glover, T. R. 1975. *The Conflict of Religions in the Early Roman Empire.* New York: Cooper Square Publishers. First published in 1909 by Methuen, London.

Grubb, Kenneth. 1947. The Relations of Church and State. *International Review of Missions* 36:142.

Gunton, Colin. 1992. Knowledge and Culture: Towards an Epistemology of the Concrete. In *The Gospel and Contemporary Culture.* Ed. Hugh Montefiore. London: Mowbray.

Hartman, Geoffrey, H. 1992. Art and Consensus in the Era of Progressive Politics. *The Yale Review* 80, no. 4 (1992): 50–61.

Hastings, Adrian. 1987. *A History of English Christianity: 1920– 1985.* London/Glasgow: Collins Fount Paperbacks.

Herbert, Robert L., ed. 1964. *The Art Criticism of John Ruskin.* New York: Da Capo Press.

Herskovits, Melville. 1948. *Man and His Works.* New York: Alfred A. Knopf.

Hocking, William Ernest. 1956. *The Coming World Civilization.* London: George Allen & Unwin.

Johnson, Paul. 1992. Eliminate the negative . . . *New York Times Book Review,* July 12.

Kant, Immanuel. 1951. *Critique of Judgement.* Trans. J. H. Bernard. New York: Hafner Press, Macmillan & Co.

Ker, Ian. 1990. *John Henry Newman.* London: Oxford University Press.

Klaaren, Eugene M. 1985. *Religious Origins of Modern Science: Belief in Creation in Seventeenth Century Thought.* Lanham, Md.: University Press of America.

Lamb, Charles, and Mary Lamb. N.d. *Tales from Shakespeare.* New York: Grosset & Dunlap.

Lawday, David. 1991. My Country Right . . . or What? *The Atlantic* 268:1.

Levenson, Jon D. 1991. The God of Abraham and the Enemies of Eurocentrism. *First Things* 15 (Oct.).

Lewis, C. S. 1954. New Learning and New Ignorance. In *Oxford History of English Literature: English Literature in the Sixteenth Century.* London/New York: Oxford University Press.

———. 1963. *Miracles: A Preliminary Study.* London/Glasgow: Fontana Books.

———. 1967. *Christian Reflections.* Grand Rapids: Eerdmans.

———. 1979. The Vision of John Bunyan. In *Selected Literary Essays.* Cambridge: Cambridge University Press.

Medawar, P. 1969. On the Effecting of All Things Possible. *The Listener* 82.

Meyer, Ernest H. 1946. *Elizabethan Chamber Music: The History of a Great Art from the Middle Ages to Purcell.* London: Lawrence & Wishart.

Mill, John Stuart. 1958. Essay on Nature. In *Nature and Utility of Religion.* New York: Liberal Arts Press.

———. 1988. Journals and Debating Speeches. In *Collected Works of John Stuart Mill.* Vol. 27. London: Routledge & Kegan Paul; Toronto: University of Toronto Press.

Newbigin, Lesslie. 1981. *The Open Secret.* Grand Rapids: Eerdmans. First published 1978.

Oman, John. 1931. *The Natural and the Supernatural.* Cambridge: Cambridge University Press.

Orwell, George. 1953. *A Collection of Essays.* New York: Harcourt Brace Jovanovich.

Pascal, Blaise. 1958. *Pascal's "Pensées."* Trans. W. F. Trotter. New York: E. P. Dutton.

Porter, Roy. 1992. What Price Gadgetry? *New York Times Book Review,* May 10.

Quiller-Couch, Arthur. 1920. *On the Art of Reading: Lectures Delivered in the University of Cambridge.* Cambridge: Cambridge University Press.

Rolleston, Thomas William. 1889. *Life of Gotthold Ephraim Lessing.* London: Walter Scott.

Russell, Bertrand. 1975. *Autobiography.* London: Unwin Paperbacks.

Ryle, Gilbert. 1990. *The Concept of Mind.* London: Penguin Books. First published in 1949 by Hutchinson & Co., London.

Schopenhauer, Arthur. 1969. *The World as Will and Representation.* 2 vols. Trans. E. F. J. Payne. New York: Dover Publications. First published 1958.

Singer, André, ed. 1981. *A History of Anthropological Thought.* New York: Basic Books.

Smith, Edwin W. 1926. *The Golden Stool: Some Aspects of the Conflict of Cultures in Modern Africa.* London: Holborn Publishing House.

Steiner, George. 1986. *Real Presences: The Leslie Stephen Memorial Lecture.* Cambridge: Cambridge University Press.

Tawney, R. H. 1966. *The Radical Tradition: Twelve Essays on Politics, Education and Literature.* London: Penguin Books.

Thomas, Keith. 1971. *Religion and the Decline of Magic.* New York: Charles Scribner's Sons.

Toynbee, Arnold. 1957. *Christianity Among the Religions of the World.* New York: Charles Scribner's Sons.

Trevor-Roper, Hugh. 1967. *Religion, the Reformation and Social Change.* London: Macmillan & Co.

———. 1985. *Renaissance Essays.* Chicago: University of Chicago Press.

Troeltsch, Ernst. 1971. *The Absoluteness of Christianity and the History of Religion.* Richmond: John Knox Press, 1971.

———. 1991. *Religion in History.* Minneapolis: Fortress Press.

Walker, D. P. 1958. *Spiritual and Demonic Magic: From Ficino to Campanella.* London: The Warburg Institute, University of London.

Westermann, Diedrich. The Place and Functioning of the Vernacular in African Education. *The International Review of Missions* 14 (Jan. 1925): 28.

Whitman, Walt. 1982. The Bible as Poetry. In *"November Boughs": Complete Poetry and Collected Prose.* New York: Library Classics of the United States.

Wightman, W. P. D. 1972. *Science in a Renaissance Society.* London: Hutchinson University Library.

Williams, Bernard. 1985. *Ethics and the Limits of Philosophy.* Cambridge, Mass.: Harvard University Press.

Wilson, F. Paul. 1989. Letter to the Editor. *New York Times Book Review,* Aug. 13.

Winckelmann, J. Joachim. 1808–25. *Werke.* Dresden: Bk IV, Ch II, #23.